NEVER GO
SHOPPING
WHEN
YOU'RE HUNGRY

SIMPLE STRATEGIES FOR
CLEAR RESULTS IN BUSINESS

By

Paul Colligan

NEVER GO SHOPPING WHEN YOU'RE HUNGRY:
SIMPLE STRATEGIES FOR CLEAR RESULTS IN BUSINESS
Copyright © 2023 by Paul Colligan

To request permissions, contact the publisher at
publish@joapublishing.com or PodcastPartnership@Gmail.com

Paperback ISBN: 978-1-961098-10-7
eBook ISBN: 978-1-961098-09-1
Printed in the USA.

Joan of Arc Publishing
Meridian, ID 83646
www.joapublishing.com

This book is so much more than just four questions.

Scan the QR Code to get access to BONUS material:

Claim Your

Never Go Shopping When You're Hungry

Power Pack: Video Training, Worksheets, and More!

http://NeverShopWhenHungry.com

Table of Contents

"Paul Colligan is one of those irreplaceable people who adds benefit with every minute you talk with him and every idea he gives you. He knows his stuff—and the time spent with him is productive."

Kathy Kolbe
Founder of Kolbe Corp

"I am so convinced of the power of a podcast that I have four of them. . . . I've hired Paul Colligan to manage all of our podcasts."

Joe Polish
Founder of Genius Network and GeniusX

"With Paul's coaching, my audience continues to grow—and they are engaged and taking action."

JJ Virgin
Celebrity Nutrition and Fitness Expert,
and Four-Time NY Times Best-Selling Author

"His courses are rock solid and the guy is super genuine."
Brendon Burchard
#1 New York Times Best-Selling Author and
"The World's Leading High-Performance Coach"

"If you want to podcast and get results, work with 'The Podmaster,' Paul Colligan. He's been podcasting since day one and will show you how to do it the right way."

Mike Koenigs
Thirteen-Time #1 Bestselling Author, Interactive Online TV Producer, Angel Investor, Filmmaker, International Speaker and Patented Inventor

CHAPTER 1

What to Do
with Your Hunger

*"It's funny in a way, or possibly sad, depending
on how you look at it, how we keep falling back
into our same silly cycles."*

That's the thought I have most often on my way home from
shopping. I would normally say, "Don't get me started,"
but here we are. *I've already started.*

If you are sick of getting stuck in busy cycles in your business
and would like clear results . . . then stick with me through this
mini book. You don't need to keep getting stuck.

Most of us know, as sure as the day is long, that if we head into
the grocery store when we are hungry and without a plan, we're
going to spend more than we need to, not eat as well as we
could, and come home with embarrassing crap that we bought
because we didn't make a simple plan. When we go into a store

hungry, and they have someone handing out samples of some promotional item, the sample person gives us a morsel of something we never knew existed, or that we ever wanted, but we come home with a big bag of it anyway. Or, even if there are no samples being given out, some other thing catches our eye on an endcap and we think it's probably a good idea, so we throw it into the cart.

Along this same line, if we are hungry and don't have a plan, it doesn't matter what store we walk into. Whether it be the latest-and-greatest upgraded Whole Foods, Costco, or a "bargain" market, it's the same thing over and over again. We wasted our time, spent too much, added crap to our inventory, and didn't get some, or most, of what we really wanted in the first place. I call it *Overactive Possibility Syndrome, or O.P.S.* for short.

If we're honest, the repercussions of this bad habit, at best, are a few wasted dollars, a less-than-perfect meal, and a forfeiture of the intended experience. If we had had a plan, and weren't hungry when we went into that market, we could be having better food, with better leftovers for the next couple of days. But no. We succumb to some elusive force, most likely comprised of impulsiveness, guilt, and adventure, and put our limited resources toward things that don't accomplish the mission. So afterward, we then arrive home with way too many bags, upset with ourselves for wasting our time, energy, and money.

But hang on, because the REAL problem is that the grocery store isn't the only place we do this. Unfortunately, O.P.S.

hides in waiting for us in many places that we don't even want to admit because the waste of time and money starts to really get embarrassing. Oh . . . we also don't get the things done that we were trying to do in the first place, and we needlessly pay more money for that particular "honor." And for those of us who are entrepreneurs, it can be more common than for others. And it can be even worse than a bad shopping trip.

Ugh!

The reason it can be worse for entrepreneurs is really quite simple. In our respective professional fields, we are singularly responsible for all the needs of our businesses. And let's face it directly: Our businesses are always *hungry*. And because our businesses are always hungry, *we* are always hungry. *Always*. We are hungry *for more*. Hungry *for accomplishment*. Hungry *for impact*. Hungry *for sales*. Hungry *for the hacks*. Hungry *for excellence*. Hungry *for results*. Hungry. Hungry. Hungry.

I know you are reading this book because you are *hungry for results*. And sometimes that hunger takes us down some pretty scary paths leading to some pretty dark places. One of the more commonly known pitfalls for the entrepreneur is *addiction*. Susceptibility to addiction among entrepreneurs is huge, partly because we are so hungry. We would do anything to keep our business, "our baby," alive. We keep crazy hours, work unusually hectic schedules, feel all the weight of responsibility to deliver for every single customer or client, keep things running in the background, and we must also plan ahead so that our baby doesn't starve in the future.

But when it comes to taking care of the needs of our business, our "fix" is never as easy as "eating something before you head to the store"—but it is where we need to start. In the sphere of running a business, O.P.S. is too big a factor to write off with a simple analogy. It's a good starting point because it helps frame the mindset, but it's not the whole enchilada. We need *another* strategy and need to know the right questions to ask before ever "entering the store" so that our "recipe" doesn't suffer as a result.

This book is that strategy—your recipe for success, if you will. It's time to start shopping with a proven plan so that the recipe will succeed by asking four key questions. We'll discover these four questions in detail in the coming chapters so that your shopping list is properly tailored to the actual needs and wants of your business.

So, let's go. . . . And let's have some eye-opening fun at the same time.

Overactive Possibility Syndrome - O.P.S.

The frenzied state of too many opportunities blocking the necessity of accomplishing the task at hand.

Example: *Yes, there are 10,000 dinners you could make after shopping at Costco. But you still have to make dinner. So, pick one.*

But before you move to the next chapter . . .

I firmly believe this is one of those things where you should start tracking your progress right away. Write it down! Please don't think you need to provide "data." That's not the point.

Even if it's just "notes" that you write down, you can come back to them later. But take the time to answer the following questions in both general and truthful statements. I think it will help you relate to upcoming pages.

So, go take a break if you need to. But when you come back, take a few minutes and write a few thoughts about a time when you went shopping and you knew you were hungry.

What did you end up buying that you didn't need?

_____

_____

_____

What did you do with the extra "stuff"?

_____

_____

_____

How much more money did that cost you?

_____

_____

_____

Once you thought about it, how did you feel about it?

_____

_____

_____

What will/should/could keep you from doing the same in the future?

_____

_____

_____

The **book** you are reading contains the *strategies* needed to effectively manage your hunger as you take on your next project. Don't worry about what to do with these strategies because the specifics are found in the recipe cards and the shopping lists.

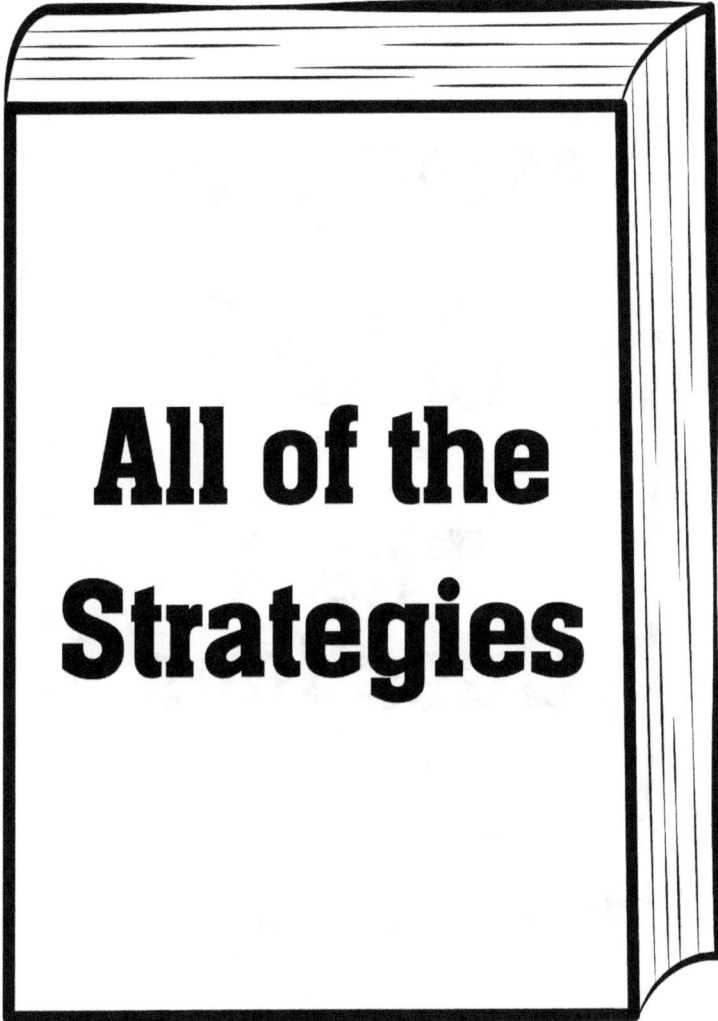

All of the Strategies

The Recipe Cards Are the step-by-step *directions* (and there aren't many of them) to take on the four simple questions that should guide everything you do.

Recipe Card

The 4 Questions

The **Shopping List** comes from you and your project. You'll need to *write out the shopping list specifically tailored to what you are doing*. We'll give you what you need to make the list as complete as possible.

Shopping List

YOU CREATE YOUR OWN
LIST BASED OFF OF
YOUR RECIPE

CHAPTER 2

Let's Play a Game

(But first, let's stop playing stupid games)

Do you remember the old game Hungry Hungry Hippos? If not, google it. Or, better yet . . . look it up on YouTube. It is a headache-inducing game of total chaos, wasted energy, obnoxious repetition, even the likelihood of carpal tunnel syndrome later in life. But, people play because in the noise, chaos, and activity of all it, they feel like they're getting something done. A lot of time spent these days is about as strategic as playing this game, which should have died before I ever entered kindergarten.

And yes, sadly, they are still selling it on Amazon.

There is nothing good about this game after your first 30 seconds playing it. Once you realize you could just grab the desired marbles and be done with it, the whole thing stops making sense—*if you can hear above the noise.* The same is true with so many online projects I see. I see so many people just pounding on their projects like a five-year-old kid, high on Kool-Aid with all of its artificial colors and flavors. *It is a truly pointless exercise in mindlessness.* Remember that last sentence. I won't repeat it, but it will define much of the playing field moving forward.

We are going to play a real game here that isn't a waste of time. There will be a real strategy, and the time spent on it with the right focus is the fastest path to "grabbing the marbles" you are hoping for with this project. No needless time spent pounding on a lever and watching everything spin around in chaos. It won't be as loud, or as fast, or as headache-inducing.

The rules are simple: Follow the steps. Reach the goal. Win the game.

So the lesson to be learned here, before we get into the meat of this book, is: Don't be part of the chaos (hunger-induced or otherwise). Don't allow it to take control of you in any way. That might be easier said than done, but once you accept a few good truths, the lessons become *tangible material* in your satchel. You can take all of that learning with you. So literally, throw your copy of Hungry Hungry Hippos away. And please, don't pass it along to someone else, not even for the tax credit. Nobody needs this.

It's time to grow up and play a real game that you can win.

It's a game in which **you can help** shape the rules. And if that's not a positive setting to build the framework for a mindset, *show me something better,* and I'll be happy to write about that in my next book.

Right now, what are you REALLY hungry for (and I'm not talking about food or drink)?

_____

_____

_____

Why are you hungry for it?

_____

_____

_____

What hunger does that hunger feed?

_____

_____

_____

When that hunger is "fed," what happens to you?

_____

_____

_____

NEVER GO SHOPPING WHEN YOU'RE HUNGRY

CHAPTER 3

I Don't Want
to Waste Your Time

Time is precious.
I promise not to waste it.
Let's keep moving forward . . .

I want to set up the presentation of this book properly so I provide context wherever needed. However, I don't want to waste your time with introductions and other details you don't need. This book is not about the people involved, but the meaningful information derived from any given situation.

Believe me. I've wasted more time than I care to admit, for myself, and a lot of other people. And that's actually a little sad. It doesn't even matter who I am; I have important things to teach you.

Before I "uncovered" or "discovered" the links between the pieces of the riddle, I personally engaged in precisely 237

"discovery calls" about podcasting, YouTube marketing, social media campaigns, and eBook production.

They would ask me all the entry-level questions about:

- What microphone should I get?

- What style of show should I have for my idea?

- How long should it be?

- Where should I host it?

- What kind of graphics should be included?

- What category should I market myself in?

- How can I market it?

- How many, and which, platforms to present on?

- What should my keywords be?

Really, I could go on. The list was predictable and seemed to go on forever. And, let's be honest, *many of these could have been answered with a simple Google search.*

In my day-to-day interactions, *EVERYONE* would thank me. And I'd get great kudos for the calls. But the underlying content of the exchange was more on the "empty" side of the gauge. And in an unfulfilling way, the only actions that could be taken from these calls were not related to my intended purpose—or results for the client on the other side.

> *These people were shopping while hungry,
> and I was feeding them the junk food they
> were reaching for.*

They didn't know what they really wanted so they asked generic questions that they felt they should ask to see what might come of it—kind of like going up and down the aisles at the grocery store looking for inspiration.

I could feel it in the fabric of the conversation itself. I actually sometimes wondered, when they hung up the phone with me, if they went back to playing Hungry Hungry Hippos.

It is nothing short of a thrill to take people through this new process. To go from "what kind of microphone should I buy?" (the hunger question) to "what are my options for tracking my success?" (the strategy question) in a single conversation is a real mind-blow. You'll be making those distinctions before you finish this book.

You're going to love it.

Although I've stopped the madness of conducting these discovery calls at our company, there are hundreds of consultants out there who would be more than willing to take you down that path. The problem with these calls was that they didn't answer any important questions. They also, almost always, resulted in a secondary stack of questions, often twice as long, that also led to nowhere.

To give you an idea of how these questions really missed the mark, let me give you a few scenarios.

- Talking about cooking techniques without knowing what you want for dinner is silly.

- Checking the sound system at the local comedy club before you have been considered for a slot is a waste of time.

- Building a video studio without knowing that this is the right medium for you is, quite simply, the wrong first step.

- Scheduling your flight for an event you don't know the dates for yet is just lost money.

- Buying books for a college class at a university that hasn't accepted you yet is time and money wasted.

- Shopping for a bathing suit with no plans for a trip to the pool or beach is taking your steps out of order.

I could go on, but I think you understand the disconnect . . .

But in reality, the problem isn't the discovery call or the wrong first step.

The real problem is this: You're about to take on some sort of project, in new territory for you, and you're not sure what's next.

You've been told there are a few hundred things you need to consider and you don't know what to do now. ***You,*** personally, are literally hungry for what's next but you find yourself in a warehouse with thousands of opportunities.

The project you are taking on could be the launch of a podcast, the "relaunch" of an unsuccessful social campaign, a social-influencer series, or something else entirely. It really doesn't matter. But your intended message is really important, and you've got this gut feeling that it might get lost in the midst of all the tech.

And like I already said, you're *hungry*.

As you "shop" for your solution, you let that hunger kick in, and you aimlessly begin buying books, equipment, technologies, microphones, upgrades, and cameras and paying for consultants, masterminds, training events . . . and way more.

> *Your hunger for the best becomes unevenly mixed with your ability to do great things with what you already have in front of you.*

This ultimately results in a proverbial shopping cart full of things that you don't need, and which take too much of what Joe Polish calls, "TAMEE." This is your Time, Attention, Money, Energy, and Effort. Certainly worth considering before walking into any market when you're planning a project, don't you think?

So, what do you do next?

The next step is to answer one simple question before you ever get near the store:

What do you want the project to do?

The rest of the process (and this book) involves answering three more questions after this one. You would do well to consider it a recipe. Or better yet, call it *your recipe*. Once you have the right answers for your recipe, the action is easy. I'll guide you to what's next.

I'll also give you the shopping list for the recipe. The more you internalize these principles, the more completely you'll appreciate the depth of their simplicity.

PS Do you want a bonus side-benefit?

Answering these questions will reduce your stress and allow you to easily work with the people who can make it happen.

They can manage the project for you, instead of you taking the more stressful and expensive path of managing a bunch of people working on a vague goal.

You don't want or need that stress.

In a past episode of the *Back To Work* podcast, Merlin Mann told a story I will never forget. He had gone through the checkout line at Costco and the clerk told him his membership card had expired and he needed to renew it. When Merlin asked when his card had expired the clerk told him, "18 months ago."

Initially Merlin wondered how that could be possible. He was there to pick up some of his favorite Costco brand items that had just run out. Was he in a time warp? No, of course not.

But then he realized he'd been using a shopping delivery service, which he loved, and they had been doing his Costco shopping for him for more than the last 18 months. Ever since then, he never really needed to go to Costco because someone else was always going for him. He would always just give them a list and then, magically, the stuff showed up at his door. And as an added bonus, he didn't even have to pay for a Costco membership. . . . Yes, there were delivery fees, but think of how much time and attention Merlin saved for 18+ months without even thinking about it. It was a source of stress that he no longer felt because his arrangement relieved him from the physical tasks and mental responsibility.

So, as you go through this book, keep this little example in mind. You never know where your thoughts will dramatically save you in your efforts, unless you write them down so you are conscious of them at the top of your mind.

So in light of this, you've probably already noticed that there are several places in this book to work out your ideas. I also have worksheets for the four questions at the end of this book. Getting clear on your answers before you go into your next project will put you so far ahead. Don't skip through answering the questions. If you take the time to answer the questions, you will no longer have to run up and down the aisles aimlessly. Heck, you might even want to buy a few copies of this book for each different project you're working on.

Yes, you read that right. This is an entirely new way of taking on a new project. Follow these steps and it truly gets easier. So, my friend, *go ahead and exhale.*

This is a book about putting your thoughts into the actions that you need to take, at the very least. Writing your thoughts down will help you build out unique recipes for each stage. This book was designed to be short because nothing about this project goes anywhere just because you are reading my fancy prose. So please, write some prose of your own in this book. *That way, we can say it's "our" book.*

In my company, the truth is, no matter how much you pay us, we won't take on any client (even the cool ones who beg) without first going through the same four questions. And as a matter of fact, that's exactly why I've written this book. Everyone needs to go through these questions.

Some of you may be thinking, "Wait a minute, Paul. Is this why you sent me the book and told me to go through it before our next call?" And my answer will be, "Yes."

Want to see results? I know . . . silly question. You're already reading this book. Here's how to do it:

Ask the four questions.

Spend as much time as needed answering them.

Launch your project based on your answers
(more on that later).

Refine as needed along the way.

I've got 13 other books under my belt. But of all the ones I've written up until now, this is the most important by far. I've shown up. *Will you?*

Let's go . . .

CHAPTER 4

Trust Me

If you are one of the people who can say you actually "know" me, you can skip this section. If you don't know me, here are a few words to set up why you can trust me in this endeavor. It's actually not about me at all. It's about our clients and what they've done, and how you can achieve the same success.

Our clients have seen millions of podcast downloads and YouTube streams. Many have reached #1 in their category (and all of Apple Podcasts) and, most importantly, can point directly to how their project fits into their larger business. They are seeing CPM rates of more than 100 times the industry average, and aren't stressed out in the process. We coach someone in podcasting that is doing 11 different podcasts at the same time, all while running multimillion dollar businesses.

Some fantastic "names" have trusted us to guide them. They include bestselling authors Brendon Burchard, J.J. Virgin, Donald Miller, Sally Hogshead, Lisa Sasevich, Frank Kern,

Joe Polish, Michael Stelzner, and others. Past projects have included work with Microsoft, StoryBrand, The US State Department, Piranha Marketing, Pearson Education, and more.

I've already mentioned the 13 other books I've written. On Amazon, most of them climbed to #1 on the day they were released. Fun fact: my first podcasting book came out over a year before the iPhone. Wacky fact: although almost 20 years old, I still get emails on a regular basis from people who read the book and loved the strategies, but wonder why I "never mentioned the iPhone" in it. They bought the book hungry.

I also speak/teach around the world on related topics. I've been given the gift of being able to refine the process with every new launch, in every book, with every client, and in every case study. It's very solid now. And as a result, I can honestly say I've been there, done that, and helped my clients buy the t-shirt.

Let's get to work, my hungry, hungry friends.

CHAPTER 5

Order of Operations

Most projects like yours, if they are doomed to fail, will most likely fail because they start in the spirit of "What should (or could) I do" versus "What do I want to do?" Far too often, people jump into a new project because "everyone else" is doing the same thing. I mean, who doesn't have a podcast these days? If "Cool Person X" is doing it, why *shouldn't* you, right? You'd be surprised at the number of times I've received a phone call and someone has asked me, "Paul, I've got my video studio all set up. What *should* I do?" And I have to point out that they have the cart before the horse. Their order of operations has a potentially fatal flaw. In the words of Tony Robbins, "Stop 'should-ing' all over yourself."

And on top of that, consultants and vendors spend your time, money, and energy on the vaguest of plans to achieve the foggiest of possible outcomes. When you don't know what you want, it's like giving your consultant "crack," especially if they bill by the hour. Then, when the project actually gets underway, you shop while hungry. As you salivate over the potential for what you could accomplish, you begin to fill your cart with every cool thing that you simply don't need.

Fire

Aim

Ready

The fix to this situation lies in knowing what you really **want** from the project. And once you know what you really want, the order of operations for the task at hand becomes easier to identify. Instead of the "Fire . . . Aim . . . Ready!" approach you're currently engaged in, which more or less equates to the "move fast and break things" spirit of so many projects, we need to start with the tried-and-true "Ready . . . Aim . . . Fire!" approach.

Ready

Aim

Fire

This should be an obvious point. And I will admit that it's easy to say that from an outsider's perspective. But the excitement and noise of our modern age often get in the way of doing things as intelligently as we are able. Everything moves so fast nowadays, we subscribe to the mentality of "Let's just act," don't we? "Action is better than inaction," right? Well, not always. And in your case, probably not. *So instead of the "Let's just act" mindset,* try this:

"Let's just ask" *four simple questions.*

Let's get the order of operations in proper sequence, so that when we do take action, we are actually taking a positive step toward our desired outcome.

So . . . the rest of this section is designed to prepare the mental landscape for your ability to address the four questions. You're probably thinking, "C'mon, Paul. . . . just get to it already."

Well, you can skip ahead if you want. I'm not holding you back. But if you want to see what I see as the proper context for your goals, please indulge me for just a little longer.

First of all, here's a not-so-little tip: *If you don't know the answers, or where to get the answers, you might not be taking on the right project.*

And sticking with the "Ready . . . Aim . . . Fire!" analogy, the first question you must ask yourself gets you "ready." Once you know what you want to do, the steps to getting it done become much easier, simply because they become more clearly defined. And there's another side-benefit that comes with the clarity in answering the first question. *It can be a bit intoxicating.* In all the good ways.

The second question is all about your "aim." Generally speaking, we start off pointed in the right direction with our sights set on what we want to do. But we have to deal with obstacles, consider a different vantage point, and determine an optimal shooting platform.

Once you are in position, the third and fourth questions steady the aim, and help you focus on precisely when and where to "fire." Always keep in mind that the precision of your efforts has an element of timing to it as well.

Admit it . . . You're excited.

And yet, somehow you're already breathing a bit more calmly and deeply because you know you're going to launch with an actual *plan*. **And it will be a *good* plan because you asked the right questions.**

Okay . . . Now consider this:

If someone were to drop you into the middle of a giant maze, could you find your way out? The short answer is, "yes." But how long would it take you? Did you know you can actually get out of any maze? Yes, it's possible. All you have to do is keep walking and never take your hand off the wall. You might have to touch every wall, and cross over where you've been before, but eventually, you will find the exit. Hurrah!

So the really important considerations here are: Which maze do I want to be in? How many walls are there? Is there only one exit? Do I have time for all of this? How can I simplify "my maze"? Let's take a look at two different question-mazes.

Here's Maze A:

What should my show be about?

What's the title?

What's the format?

Interview or monologue?

Style of edit?

Who is my editor?

What kind of microphone?

What kind of camera?

How do I monetize?

Where should I host it?

What kind of lighting?

How many episodes?

Who should I work with?

Should I do an NFT?

How long?

Should I get a website?

What should my topic be?

Social strategy?

What style of art should I use?

What is my AI strategy?

Technology required?

Remote recording platform?

What should I do?

How do I get guests?

What would work best for me?

Should I do YouTube?

Serious or fun?

Should I offshore my editing?

What is my SEO strategy?

What should I outsource?

Will my guests promote for me?

Just audio, or audio and video?

Should I have an affiliate program?

Should I do short-form content?

How many downloads should I get after 6 months?

All of those questions are the walls of the maze!

How many times will you have to double back?

How will you know if you've made a wrong turn?

How much will it *cost* you, on the time, money, and energy scale, to get out of this maze?

Now, just for fun . . .

Go ahead and pick one of the questions above which you find to be "most important." Circle it and draw a line to whichever question is the most logical next question. Circle that, and then do it again. Continue with this "lather, rinse, repeat" process for about 10 more questions. How many lines are already overlapping? Well, congratulations! You just played Hungry Hungry Hippos . . . *and lost!* And I think we already agreed to stop playing stupid games, didn't we?

So . . . Let's get real.

What are you really salivating about making here?

And here's Maze B:

What do I want the project to do?

How will I know the project is doing it?

Is the project actually doing it?

How can I do it better?

Okay . . . moment of truth here . . . which maze would *you* prefer?

CHAPTER 6

Question 1:
What Do You Want
Your Project to *Do*?

It's not about what you want to *make*. It's about what you *want from* what you're making. This difference is hugely important to the recipe for greatness. For example, you don't want a hammer to put the picture up—you want the picture on the wall to remind you of the great memories of the amazing trip you took the picture on.

What are you really trying to do here? What do you want your book, YouTube Channel, podcast, blog, or whatever to do? When you understand what you're really salivating about making, it all comes together.

You don't merely want a "podcast." There are millions of those. You want people to be so convinced about your offerings that they call and close the deal today! You don't want to write just another book for the Amazon library; you want to write the book someone buys for someone else because that book "changed their life."

Just like you need to know what recipe you're making before you enter the grocery store, you need to *really* know what you want from what you are making. Is there room to explore your options, test your theories, and see what you like? Of course there is, but then this becomes an exploratory project and you need to adjust your expectations accordingly.

Yes, things will change along the way, and Questions 3 and 4 allow for that. But if you don't know the direction you are pointed in, you'll never get close enough to make the decisions or adjustments that matter.

Recently, I have switched over to the "Mediterranean diet." That's the *plan*, but it's not what I *want*. What I *want* is for my cholesterol, and other numbers, to reflect better internal health. We'll know the results of how I'm doing in time—and trust me on this, adjustments will be made. So, I recently brought home some branzino, which is a kind of fish also known as European Sea Bass, to see what I thought. In relation to my plan, it was as exploratory as it gets, and it's actually pretty tasty, but it is not the plan. The plan remains to get those numbers down. Will I want to make branzino part of my regular diet? Yes, at least occasionally. But that's just a variable in getting those numbers down. What I want this diet to do is so much more important than any particular item I eat (or don't eat) while I'm on it.

That said, please know that it is entirely okay if what you *want* from the project is simple or "basic." I've had people say they want to do a podcast entirely to get some facetime with some big names during the interview process. That's fine, as long as you don't think "and the ads will pay all the bills." We've had someone else use the podcast to produce the raw content for a ghostwriter to write a book from. Fantastic, just don't think you're on the New York Times list now that you're doing the show. The only thing you really need to know is, and be honest, **what is it that you want?**

What do you want your project to *do*?

_____

_____

_____

What kind of project is it?

_____

_____

_____

Is it digital or physical?

_____

_____

_____

What will happen or change for you if the project does what you want it to do?

_____

_____

_____

How would that feel?

_____

_____

_____

Now that you've thought a bit more about your project, describe what you want it to do, in as few words as possible, but try to be very specific with the words you choose. You'll be glad you put that extra focus into your desired result.

_____

_____

_____

_____

_____

_____

_____

_____

_____

An Unfair Comparison of Two Stories

I'll be referring to Bob and Linda a few times, but I'm glad to introduce you to them here.

Bob wanted to start a YouTube channel to "encourage a million people to find the greatness within themselves." It's a wonderful-sounding mission statement, but it's extremely difficult to actually accomplish because other than the "million people" mentioned, nothing about it is defined with any degree of clarity. We'll talk about it more when we get to Question 2, but it also has no hope of really paying the bills unless the project is bigger than that, and has more clearly defined terms and expectations.

Quick sidenote: There's nothing wrong with "paying the bills" with your project. In fact, if you don't pay the bills with your project, there is a good chance you'll quickly get bored with it, and you'll need to find something else before you can really build the project out to what it deserves to be. In Bob's hunger for impact, he bought all the equipment, set up the studio, bought all the training programs, went to all the right events, hired a coach, practiced for weeks, and then finally released a very expensive video. It may be "free" to *start* a YouTube channel, but good editors aren't cheap.

And . . . he got 10 views.

Linda, on the other hand, had no desire to produce a podcast unless it directly affected her bottom line. She started, from day one, designing a show that "made the phone ring." She knew that when the phone rings, her team can convert one out of every three calls to an actual sale. That remains her focus even now because her podcast directly feeds her hunger for more sales.

She will never forget the first day the phone rang as a direct result of her show. She's still not sure who was more excited. Was it *her*? Or was it the listener who said, "I love your show. I can't believe I get to talk to you."?

If I'm being honest with you, I almost always initially identify with and act a lot more like Bob than I do Linda. Bob represents the world that I play in: full of possibilities and technology to leverage with the many "cool things" to put into my shopping cart. So, why shouldn't I indulge?

When you take on a new project, do you find yourself more like Bob or Linda? Why do you think that is the case?

_____

_____

_____

What could you do to change your perspective?

_____

_____

_____

Should you *indulge?*

_____

_____

_____

THE RECIPE:

- Know, specifically, what do you want the project to *do*. The clearer you are, the better your results will be.

- Don't progress until this important step is complete.

THE SHOPPING LIST:

- 1 clear objective that you can explain to someone who doesn't understand your tech or your audience. The fewer words you can use to describe your objective, the better off you will be.

- Enough time, budget, and attention to accomplish said objective. Be realistic here.

- 2 (or more) examples of others who are doing the same thing—with the same objective—successfully.

  - Substitution option: If you don't have 2 (or more) examples, do a deep dive on "why" and what will be needed to do it differently. That deep dive might take more time than this project allows. Be okay with that.

- 1 realistic inventory and budget of what you'll need to do to make it happen. This includes investments and others who can help you do the things you don't do. No, you can't buy people, but you sure can rent their time.

While you are pondering your objective (the "what" of that first question), think about that shopping list for a *specific menu*. Ignore O.P.S. as described earlier in this book. "I want to eat Italian", although sounding nice, is without any real focus or attention. And it is nowhere near "I want enough pizza and Chianti for a table of eight, with the freshest ingredients possible and three different toppings for each pizza."

When you examine your objective, make sure to distinguish between "your desired outcome," and "you, the person delivering it." With the pizza and Chianti example above, you know that you aren't going to make and bottle the wine yourself, but you should also ask yourself, "what's more important . . . pizza and Chianti for eight? Or, you in the kitchen trying to make it happen?" I won't even go into the steps of creating a great bottle of Chianti.

I mentioned earlier the need for someone who doesn't understand what you're doing, or anything about your tech or audience. And I don't think this can be underestimated, but a good, general, rule of thumb is that if you can explain it to your team, parents, and your kids, and they all "get it" you're in a really great place. If you are still too young for kids, then explain it to your parents and grandparents. You get the idea. Anyway, getting those individuals involved is a true, hidden "shortcut" to making sure you *really* know what you **want**.

I'm sure you noticed that one of the line items on the shopping list is to identify two or more examples of others who are doing something similar to your intended vision.

This is key.

Until your objective is clearly defined, some of your thoughts are still just ideas because they aren't ready to become things yet. To illustrate this, I'll stretch the pizza analogy a little further with this: Before you go all out on serving cauliflower-crust pizza to a group of your friends, you may want to actually taste it and make sure it's something you would be proud to feed your guests. It might sound like a great idea at first. You may even be presold on the whole trend toward gluten-free foods. But the actual product may disappoint you. Before you speak of a world with amazing-tasting cauliflower crust, *make sure that such a world actually exists.*

I understand the desire and/or "need" to believe you are going to be the one who succeeds with an idea where all others have failed, but it's time for a little honesty. It probably failed for others because it wasn't such a good idea in the first place. I made allowances in the shopping list for some deep work on why the idea had failed in the past. If you're going to attempt that, be prepared to take on a pretty big project. In fact, you will almost certainly find it to be many times bigger than the actual project you want to embark upon. Just be honest about how long the real research will take, and determine if it is worth the effort.

Another element on your shopping list is a full and complete inventory (and the best budget you can allow at the time). This is also key. Yes, in today's world you can get fresh tomatoes just about anywhere for a few bucks, but the *pizza oven* needed to get the crust to your desired state of perfection might be another story altogether. If you're fine with throwing your creation on the same pan your kids attempted chocolate chip cookies on last week, that's fine; just don't expect spectacular results.

And now, we need to talk about something awkward . . .

If you are honest with yourself, what we say we want from the project and what we really want are often two different things. My friend Mike Koenigs once made the issue crystal clear to me with a simple anecdote. He said that whenever he hosts a dinner party, in an attempt to be a good host, he always asks people what they're into eating. Nearly all of them will say they're eating "healthy." When they arrive and there are different kinds of appetizers, including healthy ones and not-so-healthy ones, guess what always gets eaten first? It becomes immediately clear that people do not always mean what they say. The grocery store isn't the only place they reach for the crap if it's available. Who doesn't show up to a dinner party hungry?

In turn, many people will say, "I just want to get my book out there." Or, "I just want to share my thoughts and see what happens." Underneath those statements though, what they honestly want is to be a New York Times bestseller or the next Joe Rogan. They're a little embarrassed to say it out loud, but it's what they're really thinking.

Be brutally honest with yourself with this first of the four questions. It is the keystone to the rest of the plan. Trust me on this—the more honest you are with yourself at the very beginning, the better your results will be. If you're not sure if the goal is attainable, it might be smart to bring on someone who can tell you if it is. I'm sure that you already know this, but at this stage, you're not looking for a "mindset coach." You're looking for someone who has done it before and can tell you honestly what it will take for you to get there. So, be brutally honest with yourself here. Everybody will win when you do. And it will help determine what the *"real" win is.*

If you are being honest with yourself, and nobody else needs to see this page other than you, what do you really *want* from this project?

_____

_____

_____

There is nothing wrong with wanting. We just need to be honest with what this would really entail. Getting a book live on Amazon and having a New York Times bestseller are two completely different things.

What would it really take to get what you really want?

_____

_____

_____

Would it be better to bring on someone, now, who can help you determine if this is even possible?

_____

_____

_____

Are you able to do that?

_____

_____

_____

If you aren't, how can you adjust your "want"—or should you kill the project now?

_____

_____

_____

As my friend Alex Mandossian says, "The only thing worse than singing the wrong song is signing it loudly."

Okay . . . One more awkward moment.

An abrupt, quick reality check . . .

What if you really just don't know what you want the project to do? What if you feel like you need to start something, but you just don't know why? What do you do then? Will this book even work for you?

Well, here's where I suggest that not knowing can actually be a gift.

If you think you want to start a project—maybe even *"should"* start a project—and you can't answer the simple question of what you really want the project to do, you've just done yourself a huge favor. This should be a massive STOP sign as you're screaming down the highway warning that you were maybe shopping while hungry.

Use that STOP sign to promise yourself that you won't go a step further until you have the answer.

And if you don't know how to get that answer, *kill the project.*

Follow this simple process and you'll save yourself untold hours and dollars in wasted time and effort.

Question 1: What Do You Want Your Project to *Do*?

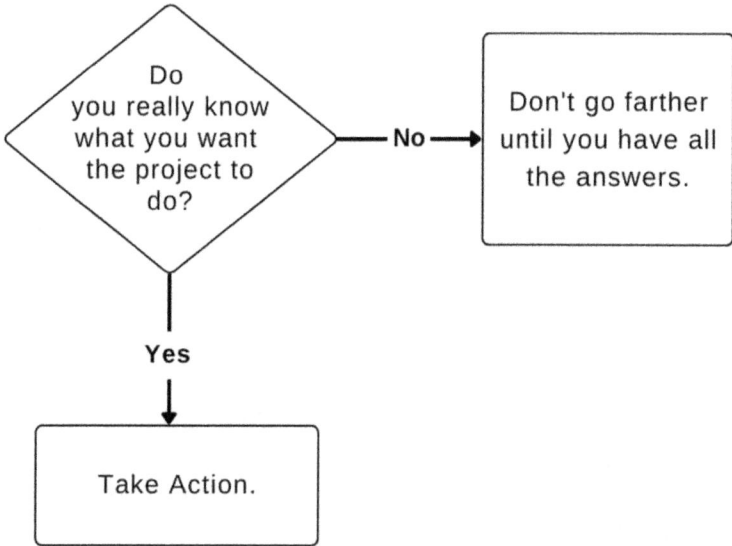

```
        ┌─────────────────┐
        │   Do            │
        │ you really know │──── No ───▶  ┌──────────────────┐
        │ what you want   │             │ Don't go farther │
        │ the project to  │             │ until you have all│
        │      do?        │             │  the answers.    │
        └─────────────────┘             └──────────────────┘
                │
               Yes
                │
                ▼
        ┌─────────────────┐
        │ Take Action.    │
        └─────────────────┘
```

CHAPTER 7

Question 2:
How Will You *Know*
That the Project Is Doing It?

It's just not enough to have a plan. You need to know if the plan is working. While some people will always have the attitude of "we'll see when we get there," the successful ones know what "there" looks like long before they even begin the trek. I've been in meetings with people who have achieved millions of views or downloads who can tell me their strategy as if Grandma herself had needlepointed it on a pillow they sleep on every night. But when I ask, "How's the plan working?" they shrug their shoulders hoping the numbers all work out in the end. This proves the point that if you don't know what you're looking for, you simply aren't going to find it (without a huge amount of dumb luck).

We'll continue to use the example of Bob and Linda throughout our examination of the four questions.

Bob desperately wants to know that he's doing a good job in his videos. He knows that no matter how hungry he is, it *takes time* to build an audience. But, Bob figures that getting some likes and positive comments on his videos will *finally* give him the encouragement he needs.

He even asks for these out loud in his presentations. And good news came pretty quickly because Bob woke up one morning to a like and a glowing comment. The bad news is that it was from Bob's mom.

In contrast, Linda's entire revenue stream comes from making the phone ring. People call to ask about her services (she's in the financial arena), and if it turns out to be a right fit, they start working together. She's designed the show in such a way that the majority of people who call are a right fit, so her conversion levels are high. She is an expert at getting to the sale and lets nothing stand in her way. She also doesn't waste any time asking things like how they heard about her. Nope. . . . She goes right for the sale.

When Linda records the podcast, she gives out a cell phone number so she can distinguish what leads come from the show versus other sources. Sometimes, obviously, the calls go to voicemail (they come in at different times during the day and night) but a call back works fine. All of her other marketing ventures make the regular business line ring. She recently realized that the cell phone rings more often than her business line does. And although her podcast is in no way "cheap," in terms of results, it costs far less than any of her other marketing efforts. *And, the podcast is a lot more fun.*

This little twist of giving out a different number for the podcast versus other marketing efforts is a really simple hack to answer that question "is the show doing it?" If all of her marketing resulted in all calls coming in on the same phone line, it would be hard to know what came from what. Yes, they could ask people how they heard about her during the initial sale, but they wanted to get right to the conversion of these "hot leads." The $25 a month spent to get right to the sale is money well-spent, indeed.

It's okay to change your mind about what you're looking for as the journey progresses, but it is a really bad strategy to go in without something specific in mind from the onset. Just don't be in a place where you need to shrug your shoulders about the key elements of your plan. It's one of the most difficult and painful places you could ever be because the weight of your time and money already spent makes that place very unpleasant.

Before you ever launch the project, you need to know what success looks like. This isn't an issue of perfection. Most likely, you won't answer this question with a clear *win* on your first try. But you will know **if** you're pointed in the right direction. And knowing if you're pointed in the right direction will make it easier to determine if you need to make a change of course along the way.

What needs to happen for you to know that your project is working in the way you intended?

_____

_____

_____

What metric will you track?

_____

_____

_____

Is it the right metric?

_____

_____

_____

Is that metric good enough to really assess the success of the project?

_____

_____

_____

Are there other metric options for you to track?

_____

_____

_____

So . . . don't take too many leaps between Questions 1 and 2. This is where Bob failed.

The idea that his audience will provide likes and comments on his videos assumes a number of things that *shouldn't be assumed*. Perhaps the audience is so inspired that they want to act, not respond. Perhaps they think Bob is already aware of how awesome he is and don't want to waste his time. Of course, the other option is that the reason they aren't responding is that they aren't inspired enough to do even that.

Linda's metric of a phone ringing, minus spam calls of course, is nearly perfect. People who want more of what she has to offer will call. "No calls" quickly equates to "nobody wants more from Linda," and that her show isn't doing what she wants it to do.

Great knives don't make anyone "a great chef."

There are too many other layers of knowledge and experience behind greatness in the culinary arts.

It doesn't matter what guitar I buy, I will never be able to "shred" like Eddie Van Halen. Similarly, great microphones don't make anyone the next Elvis, Paul McCartney, or Lady Gaga. To carry this analogy even further, *it doesn't matter how great my piano is, I'm no Mozart!*

As I type this, I am acutely aware that *no matter how good the keyboard I type on is, and no matter how fast I type, I'll simply never be the next Hemingway.*

If you know what you really want, it automatically becomes a lot easier to achieve than you might think. On the one hand, Linda's phone ringing metric is very easy to track and define. When it's easy to track and define, it's easy to build.

Sadly, Bob, on the other hand, will likely be stuck for a long time. I admire the goal to an extent, but it's too hard to define and make sense of in any monetizing way. In the back of this book, I'll give you some options for looking more closely at something like this. But regardless, one goal is much easier to track than the other. And at the risk of repeating myself, the **clearer you know what you want your project to do, the better chance you have that your project is going to accomplish it.**

Make sure you are tracking the *right* thing. In Bob's case, tracking downloads is a pretty low-level metric. If he gets a million streams of his 60-minute videos but everybody hangs up after watching a minute, that is the farthest thing away from the win.

So, let's take a look at a few more thoughts on The Recipe and the Shopping List. **Here we go:**

THE RECIPE:

- Determine exactly what you will examine to see if the project is "working" or not.

- Understand how you will eliminate the false positives of a "like" from Mom.

THE SHOPPING LIST:

- A metric for tracking that truly matters to what you are trying to accomplish.

  - Downloads mean nothing if they only listen or watch for 10 seconds.

  - Subscribers to an email newsletter only matter if they open your emails.

  - An eBook that you give away for free needs something else to define value.

- Clear directions on what, how, and when you'll track.

  - This needs to be easy for anyone involved in the project to follow.

Your goal for answering Question 2 for the first time is to do it as quickly and as honestly as possible. After that, you'll want to develop a regular habit of asking Question 2 as many times as you can. With every minor adjustment to your production, the sooner you can ask Question 2 again, the easier the adjustments will be.

For our clients, part of our monthly report is a simple analysis of whether the project is meeting the metric we set.

I have a dear family member who, bless her soul, loves to cook but always follows the recipe *exactly* as described—much to her detriment. You'd smell something burning in the oven and upon suggesting that she might want to "check," she'd look you straight in the eyes and with nothing but love in her heart say, "but the recipe says five more minutes."

And if you find yourself in a pinch . . .

You might have to change some of the specifics along the way. Don't worry. That's okay. Take it in stride and just pay attention to your resources. Use the best of what you have, and don't try to do too much with too little. In the end, it makes for a far superior product.

For example . . . Let's say you're making a show, and you've been thinking all along that 20 minutes will be the perfect length. However, shortly before your intended publishing time, you sadly realize that you only have about 10 minutes of content. **DO NOT** stretch things out because the original plan called for 20 minutes. You won't be able to "dance" your way through it to keep people engaged with your message.

Quality, credibility, reputation, and ultimately, character are all at risk.

It's not worth it.

If you have to release the show right away, focus on the ingredients you have and make a great appetizer instead of a bad dinner.

Maybe you thought that people would want to sign up for your email newsletter. However, you have realized that before they give you their email address, they want more information and specifics of what's *in* the newsletter. You see, they are in the same marketplace as you. The difference is, they are shopping and you are selling. They want to know more about your product before they commit. So never forget that "they" are "your" marketplace. Figure out what they want, and let them know you have it for them.

If discoveries or changes are made that require you to go back to the drawing board, or perhaps on another shopping run, that's okay. Discovering a necessary change now is better than finding out when doubling back will be even more costly. I've included a little story below of a great example of this.

One of the most successful podcasts, which was created by one of my favorite people in the business, started out as a 20-minute, heavily edited production. She realized she didn't have the time to do the show as originally designed and transitioned to a five-minute monologue. She did this just before attempting to record what was only her third episode. And in fewer than 10 episodes after that change, which is less than one single hour of podcast content, she was on the Oprah Winfrey Show.

She now runs a podcast network.

What is it that you should be tracking?

_____

_____

_____

How can you track it?

_____

_____

_____

Is that "enough" to tell that it is truly working?

_____

_____

_____

Is there something else that you'd be tracking if you "could"? Are you certain that it can't be tracked?

_____

_____

_____

Is it time to bring in someone else to make sure you are tracking the right thing?

_____

_____

_____

CHAPTER 8

Question 3:
Is the Project Actually Doing It?

I remember it like it was yesterday. I was only seven years old, and I was eating dinner at Fisherman's Wharf in San Francisco with my family, and my Uncle Jerry. I thought he was the coolest thing ever (and he was). And that was even *before* "the incident," which I will briefly explain here. And before I go on, I sincerely hope you have an "Uncle Jerry" in your own in life. It's not because of money, or anything along those lines. No, it's about really knowing what you want and not being afraid to ask for it.

Anyway . . .

When the wine came, he and the waiter engaged in that seemingly choreographed "tasting thing" that you often see in the movies. You know, they open the bottle, pour a little into the taster's glass and expect a compliment. Honestly, I had no idea that it was a real thing, *until that very moment*. Jerry tasted the wine and politely said, "Nope. It's corked. Send that one back. May we please have a different bottle?"

He didn't "deal with it." He didn't think "well, they're trying hard." He knew what he wanted, and this wasn't it.

They did the show I had only seen on screen. They did it all fancy (at least for a seven-year-old), and Uncle Jerry sent that back for another one.

He knew what he wanted when he ordered it, but that bottle of wine just wasn't it. Something was wrong. . . . and he certainly wasn't paying for corked wine.

And just like that . . . poof! Mind blown. From that moment on, I had a new respect for asking yourself, "Is this what I really want?"

So . . . do you want the ability to determine, immediately, if your expectations have been met? Do you want the ability to see around the next corner? Are you willing to speak up, even under pressure when everyone else is acting like everything is okay?

Is your project doing what you want it to do, or are you pushing the Hungry Hungry Hippos' knobs as quickly as possible, hoping nobody is noticing how you are doing amid all the noise?

_____

_____

_____

How do you know how your project is doing what you want it to do?

_____

_____

_____

Could you be misreading anything here?

_____

_____

_____

What are some possible misreads that you should look out for?

_____

_____

_____

Is there someone you can double-check things with?

_____

_____

_____

Bob interviewed a number of consultants and services who bumped up his online video views. It wasn't cheap, and it took a while to realize this was an option. But his numbers certainly got higher. How "real" these numbers were was a question he had in the back of his head, but he wasn't going to bring that up when things were looking so good.

Stemming from a desire to make his episodes better, he decided to look at how deep his audience was going into his videos. He figured that if he got a million streams of his videos, but everyone hung up five minutes in, that was hardly a win.

He found out that most viewers stay in his videos for less than a minute. The consultant didn't mention this point as the numbers kept going up. Are they "real" (or "bots") or are they maybe not the "right" audience? Bob can't imagine a world where someone watches 47 seconds of his 20-minute inspirational videos. Something is definitely wrong. Bob still wants to inspire millions, but he has a dark feeling in his gut.

Linda ran the numbers. For every 1,000 views or downloads of her show, she gets a phone call. She closes one out of every three phone calls. Her issue isn't closing. Rather, her focus is on getting the right people to call. Yeah, this is working for Linda. She has one question now: how do we get more people in her demographic to listen to this show? Because every download is essentially worth $3. She *has a budget to work with.*

Notice what different places Bob and Linda find themselves in. Bob has little certainty about his circumstances, while Linda knows exactly what comes next.

Which place would you rather find yourself in?

While you contemplate that option, let's briefly catch up with our Recipe and Shopping List.

THE RECIPE:

- Have someone not emotionally involved in the project outcome check the results up against your metric.

  - If you can do it, great. If you need someone else, that's okay too, and you'll probably get better data. This is your baby. Not everyone can truly check the metrics on their own project. If you can't, don't feel bad.

- This is the kind of thing consultants are great at if you don't have the right person on your team to take on the task. If the person fears telling you the truth, find someone else to tell you the truth.

- Carefully measure your answer to Question 2 with the honesty and integrity the answer deserves.

- Determine if the next step is to change something or to stop something.

THE SHOPPING LIST:

- A regular report by someone not too emotionally invested in the outcome (at least monthly) on whether or not your project is in fact reaching the stated goal.

  - It could be automated, delegated, outsourced, or done entirely by hand.

  - Just be able to answer the question quickly, based on facts.

It doesn't matter how much you *want* the project to work. It doesn't matter how dear the project is to your heart. And let's say it again: it doesn't matter how *hungry* you are. What matters is, *is this working?*

To give you a little dash of perspective, with a pinch of comic relief, here are two quotes that help summarize the point. The first is one you've most likely heard before:

> *The definition of insanity is doing the same thing over and over again and expecting different results.*

This one is attributed to Albert Einstein. Compare that to the quote I mentioned earlier:

> *The only thing worse than singing the wrong song is singing it loudly.*

The introspection we are looking for in this situation is closer to Alex's statement than Einstein's. I do, in fact, want you to sing your song, as loud as you can, until THE MOMENT you realize it is not the right song to be singing and then immediately change songs. Close your mouth if you need to. It doesn't take a brain like Einstein's to realize that if his audience wasn't watching more than a minute of his videos, Bob was singing the wrong song, and he was doing it very *loudly.*

Don't go on to Question 4 if the answer to Question 3 is simply, "no." If it is "no," we have one of two options to consider.

Option 1 - You didn't do it right.

When she was about 10, my daughter Paige noticed that whenever we put something in the oven on broil, it came out a lot quicker than it did when we put something on bake. One evening, I had just come home with a take-and-bake pizza and she was hungry (and loves pizza—who doesn't?). I told her to set the oven to 350. She figured, *why not set it to 500 on broil?* Her pizza would come faster that way, right?

Although her end product came out completely inedible, there was nothing wrong with the precooked pizza at all. She simply could have made it better by following the directions.

Sometimes the solution is that easy.

Sometimes it isn't.

You know the difference between the two.

Are you brave enough to admit it?

As soon as you notice it's not working, the very first question you need to ask is "why." If it's just a bad idea, **stop**. If it's the "wrong song," **stop**. But if it's because someone didn't follow the directions correctly, you also know what to do now.

Sometimes you are too close to realize what the problem is. Trust me on this one; there is no better fix than spending some time having someone who knows what they're doing looking at this issue for you.

If what you were trying to do wasn't done correctly, stop and do it correctly this time. You may have to throw out a whole pizza but it sure beats "singing louder."

Sometimes it isn't as clear as a charred pizza heap. If you need someone to come and determine if it was done correctly—do it now, before you waste any more time and money.

If it was done correctly, and you didn't see the results you were looking for, you only have one option.

Option 2 - You need a "redo."

If you hoped your show would get people to sign up for your email newsletter (your answer to question 2), and after 5,000 downloads not a single person has done so, *you need a redo.*

If you were sure your topic would bring you thousands of views because your audience was "looking" for it, and your view count is less than 10, *you need a redo.*

If the offer at the end of the book was supposed to get people to call you and the only calls you get are spam, *you need a redo.*

You get the idea. And you, my friend, know if you need a redo or not.

Redoes aren't bad, especially if you catch them early in the process. The sooner you catch the need to redo, the sooner you can start the process.

What to redo is simple:

If your product isn't doing what you want it to do, fix it so that it does.

or

Rewrite your answer to question 2 to be more realistic. (Now that you know what you know, you can do that.)

or

Kill the project before it takes any more of your time or money.

CHAPTER 9

Question 4:
How Can I Do It Better?

I have been roasting my own coffee for the last couple of years. The first cup of coffee I made from my own beans was pretty good. But it was really just a first step for what was to come. Since then, I've been experimenting with the right beans, from the right country, from the right region of the country (I kid you not), with the right temperature. I've got nearly 100 pages of notes tucked away in my iPad and I'm constantly improving the process.

Earlier today my wife, Heidi, said, "Wow, the coffee is good this morning," Yes, I did something different. It was a small change, but it was worth it. The cup of coffee this morning was probably 10 times better than that first cup from the first batch a few years back. A change here, a change there, and it keeps getting better. That first cup was "good"; this morning's was excellent.

The moral here is: **don't stop when your first episode is launched.**

Keep getting better.

My coffee keeps getting better because I adjust as needed. I try a slight change in temperature, timing, beans, etc. and track what works and what doesn't. If I make a desirable change, I keep going. If I don't, I switch back and start over where I made that change.

I see so many podcasts and YouTube shows that never change from the first episode to see what they can do better. It's actually quite sad. What you know after 5, 25, 100, 1000 episodes is so much more than you know when you started the process. It would be a waste of your effort to write the recipe once and never change a thing.

Just like I do with my coffee, keep track of what you're doing, make changes accordingly, and it will keep getting better and better.

Don't just set it and forget it. Do it, track it, and make it better. Your project is worth it—and so is your audience.

In a burst of inspiration after watching yet *another* YouTube guru, Bob decided that before he goes "big" with full YouTube videos, he should go for smaller and shorter content. He *again* paid an editor to cut down the content into little snippets. He pays *another* consultant to put the content everywhere that will accept it. He outsources these because they aren't what he would normally spend time on. And he's fine with that. That's a good strategy, right?

He now has views in the hundreds of thousands, according to the platforms themselves. But his videos are around 30 seconds each, not the 20 or so minutes he originally envisioned. That 30-second time frame is not Bob's choice. It's simply what those platforms require and what his consultant put out there.

Bob isn't very sure that he can encourage people to their inner greatness in only 30 seconds. Actually, he knows it isn't working, as surely as Uncle Jerry knew the wine was bad. **He just feels like he has "so much invested" that he can't change anything right now.**

Have you ever felt that way?

He's also not very sure if he's into doing his show anymore.

When you put a cake in the oven, you know you want that cake—the kind of cake you want, the flavor it should be, etc. You've set the thermostat, are smelling the goodness, and are ready for the final product. There comes a time where you need to put a toothpick into the cooking cake to see if it is in fact done. If it comes out covered in raw batter, it needs some more time. You want to finish well.

And, when the cake is done and eaten, you might ask the family what they thought of the cake. Should it have less sugar or more sugar? Did they like the addition of the Mexican Cinnamon or should we do without next time? Yes, you made the cake, somewhat successfully, but you want to make it better next time.

This is the whole role of Question 4. You can, and should, improve over time. Get better with every episode, every book, and every project.

THE RECIPE:

- Figure out what you are going to do differently next time.

  - If your project is a success, enjoy the fruits of your labor, but consider how it could be even better. Imagine what is possible with a little more focus.

  - If your project is less than a success, figure out what you need to make it better.

- Do it differently next time.

THE SHOPPING LIST:

- Write down clear steps as to what you're going to do differently next time.

How can you do it better?

_____

_____

_____

Is it about refining something? Getting more downloads? More sales?

_____

_____

_____

Is the very thing you need to do to make it better the same thing you were hoping the project would do? Or is it something different?

_____

_____

_____

What would it mean to you if it got better?

_____

_____

_____

Who would be the right person to help you do it better?

_____

_____

_____

Linda's show works for *her*, not the other way around. She pays for real downloads whenever she can get them, as long as they cost her less than a dollar each. While that machine is in place, and very profitable, she's now working on getting even more people on the show to call her. She's refining her content the same way I'm working on my coffee.

Bob tried to refine his approach the only way he could. Although he says that he wants to "inspire millions," deep down, he really wants to do that by being a YouTube star. He really couldn't go in any direction other than the one he went. At some point in time, I'm sure he'll be pulling the plug on this process, or hiding the loss with that classic line "I know half of my marketing budget is working; I just don't know which half."

Linda, on the other hand, has a machine now. She knows what she wants the show to do, she knows how to do it, she knows how much she can spend doing it and she now has the glorious task of just making things better.

I discovered the wonderful world of roasting coffee at home during the COVID lockdowns. I always knew I wanted to give this a try, and I certainly had plenty of time on my hands to make it happen. I started with some random beans of unknown origin (they came with the roaster, which was really nothing more than a glorified hot-air popcorn popper), as well as some idea in my head that the darker I roasted the beans, the tastier the coffee in my cup would be. I ordered the necessary equipment along with a whole bunch of beans, and I filled my journal with over a hundred pages of notes. And then I noticed something fascinating beginning to emerge. I *really liked* the taste of coffee when it had been roasted to a much lesser degree than a full dark roast. And I know from asking Questions 3 and 4 over and over again that I prefer beans not only from a particular country, but a specific region in that country.

I now roast and drink what I call my "special reserve." In fact, I'm enjoying a cup of it right now, exactly the way I like it. Strangely enough, I've become so obsessed with these results that I actually now travel with my freshly roasted beans, a hand grinder, and a brewing device called the Aeropress. At first, I simply wanted to try my hand at coffee roasting. Would I even like it? Would I drink it? Would it be worth the effort? Would it be good enough for others? I've come a long way since then. But because I tracked everything along the way, I now know the perfect bean for my pallet as well as the perfect temperatures for this kind of bean. It truly came down to following "my recipe," asking the right questions along the way, and making the necessary adjustments for improvement.

I could have stuck with the taste and style of that first roast, but I'm sure glad I didn't.

How do you *feel* about the way that you answered question 4?

_____

_____

_____

Were you honest with yourself and the numbers?

_____

_____

_____

Are there other possible answers?

_____

_____

_____

Who could you ask to help you deal with the results?

_____

_____

_____

What if you can't answer the questions to your liking?

Sometimes the project isn't doing what you want. Sometimes there is no way to do it better. Sometimes it will never be good enough. This is tough, but it's a reality that we need to think about and deal with. Believe me, I've tried, way too many times, to make a pizza crust from cauliflower that would actually taste good. But I had to get honest with myself and just face the fact that cauliflower will NEVER taste like a traditional pizza crust.

What do I do with a *hard* fact when I come across it?

I have a friend with a podcast for a fairly niche audience that "only" gets a quarter of a million downloads every episode. I've told him repeatedly that this is almost the entirety of his market, yet he wants to push for more downloads. Of course, he wants his show to get as many downloads as possible so he can sell as many ads as possible. Personally, I have no problem with him *wanting* this. But professionally, the simple fact is that he won't be getting more (legit) downloads. He has reached the end of his line. Those are just the facts—and he isn't being personally honest with them. When you reach this point, there are three paths.

- *Path 1: Be satisfied with what you have.* Those 250,000 downloads generate a nice little chunk of change for the show mentioned previously. It just won't generate more. As long as my friend doesn't spend more producing the show than he makes, he can enjoy this profit center for a long time and have a blast while doing it. It just might not have the number associated with it that he wanted.

- **Path 2**: *Make some deep changes.* My friend's show is extremely niche. He could increase the niche a bit and get a bigger audience for which he could sell more ads. Personally, I don't think the show would be nearly as good, but sometimes you need to make some deep changes.

- **Path 3**: *Abandon the project.* I don't know who to attribute this phrase to, but a question I ask over and over is, "is the juice worth the squeeze?" Sometimes it isn't. It is never easy to come to that realization, but sometimes you just have to.

Is the "juice worth the squeeze" in the project right now?

_____

_____

_____

If it is, what do you need to get more fruit to squeeze?

_____

_____

_____

Is it affordable?

_____

_____

_____

What would need to change for it to be affordable?

_____

_____

_____

**Is that something you could do yourself?
Do you know how to do it?**

_____

_____

_____

Is there someone who could help you?

_____

_____

_____

CHAPTER 10

Through the Questions
One More Time

Please don't keep doing the same thing over and over, hoping for different results. Go through the four-question process, as many times as you need to, with honest intent to avoid the pitfalls of not having a plan, a recipe, and a shopping list. When you move from grabbing a bunch of cool things and throwing them in your cart, to a carefully crafted plan for why you're entering the store in the first place, it dramatically changes your results as well as your experience of achieving that outcome.

Question 1 gives you the focus you need to give you the highest chance at success. I would never tell you that success comes from the perfect implementation of your initial attempt to answer **Question 1**. But I will also tell you that **Questions 2, 3, and 4** give you the flexibility to adjust and make changes when you need to. And of these, **Question 2** is perhaps my favorite. It provides the simple truth that if you don't know what a win looks like, you'll never win. We hungry types will continue to play whatever game is in front of us. But when we know what results we actually want, as well as what we want from those results, the whole project and the whole journey become more enjoyable and truly fulfilling.

I have seen countless books written, social media posts syndicated, podcasts published, YouTube videos promoted, and plenty of other endeavors that, although they took a lot of time (and look fancy, fancy, fancy), they clearly had no end game. At best, they get a sigh. There is also a mentality of "fake it till you make it" that has many people launching without a real goal of what the win means, and they hope that they'll figure out success along the way. If success lands in your lap under such conditions, congratulations.

Just never pretend it was a strategy.

A clear win with no way to track how it happened is no win at all; it's dumb luck, and very uncommon. You have to know when to call "victory." You'd be surprised who simply doesn't have that capacity. No matter how good the dream or the plan may be, if you don't know how to identify the victory when it happens, you can't repeat the process or avoid future problems with what you already have going. Those people who can't answer the question of how they will know if the project is "doing it" know deep in their gut that they *should* be doing something. They know the project is sucking away their time and money while also taking away from the stuff that matters even more.

This might hurt, but there is simply no correlation between the success of your project and the time and money you've spent on it so far . . .

This is why **Question 3** is so key. If you aren't willing to check to see if the "plan" is, in fact, working, the chances are pretty strong that it isn't. I would actually suggest that if you don't find time, effort, or sometimes even the budget to look at this question, then you probably already know deep down that, in fact, it isn't working and you just don't want to face the facts.

I know I said **Question 2** is perhaps my favorite, but **Question 4** is the most important one. Making it better is the key to seeing real success from your project. The mission you embark on, and a win in year one, might be enough for year one. But if you could do better in year two, and do it again in year- three and beyond, why wouldn't you? The process of making it better will actually restart the whole cycle. So if it's working, push to make it work better.

I live in Portland, Oregon. We take our coffee seriously here. The never-ending rain means we need a source of never-ending caffeine. Coffee tends to be how we do it, and we do it very well. We are hungry for that hit. You may not know a Portlander's hunger for a strong cup of coffee to get out of that Portland Funk, but you do know a hunger of your own that would easily compare.

I already told you a bit about my coffee-roasting hobby, and I can tell you this: It's the best coffee I've ever had. And in the end, I pay less than half per pound for what I would be able to obtain locally for an "acceptable" choice from a local roaster. I drink exactly what I want. I drink it exactly the way I want. And it keeps getting better. My coffee, my terms, and my desired results.

When I order those beans, I don't just log onto the website and grab something that sounds fun. I know exactly what I want, and I get it. I'm in and out in a few minutes and the UPS driver delivers 50 pounds of green coffee like clockwork. I love the process because I know what it will produce. And it's not just me blowing my own horn. No, I roast coffee for a number of other families because they too won't settle for the "normal stuff." I even trade coffee for eggs with a friend who raises some kind of organic-artisan-super-fancy-pants chickens, so my breakfasts are just fantastic. And all this comes with minimal effort—and a lot of fun.

You can have that same feeling on whatever project you are taking on.

I've created such a wonderful routine over it, it's almost embarrassing how I can almost fly out of bed in the morning because I know the cup of coffee that is waiting for me on the other side. When you are always looking at making it better, you are living in a world, as Dan Sullivan says, "where your future is bigger than your past." That reality alone will give you more energy than even one of my cups of coffee.

The first book I ever wrote was for someone else who told me what the book was supposed to contain. It was basically a big, boring, technical book, but on the other hand it was a ghostwriting gig that actually paid quite well, so I took it on.

Should I make the "I was young and foolish" joke here?

I learned pretty quickly that this wasn't really "my thing." I was able to get through the motions, but it just wasn't "me." The point to be made here is that you need to make this *your project on your terms*. And now you have these questions, or at least know how to work directly with the person who will get you the answers.

So, make sure you do all of this the way *you know it needs to be done*. I promise you, part of the hunger you feel lies in not being able to do the project on your terms. Hopefully, this book changes that so you can get right to it.

What is a project in your past that you did on someone else's terms?

_____

_____

_____

How did that make you feel? What were the results?

_____

_____

_____

What would you have done differently?

_____

_____

_____

How does the idea of being in charge of this next project feel to you?

_____

_____

_____

CHAPTER 11

Your New Energy Source

Now that you are reaching the last few pages of this book, you may be thinking that the title of this book is a bit of a misnomer. And I would say that's actually a fair criticism. As an entrepreneur in the real world, you will always be hungry when you are shopping for your business.

But now that you understand the purpose of the four questions, and how they are designed to prevent the unnecessary waste of your time and money, you should be able to deal with it like *a pro with a purpose.*

Moving forward, you can now shop with an effective plan that will help prevent the pitfalls of what can often be a pointless exercise in mindlessness. And once you discover that all the frustrations associated with shopping hungry no longer threaten your plan, you will be able to navigate your way to your desired results, even if you have to change direction along the way.

Imagine waking up in the morning with an energetic bounce in your step because you know exactly what you want from your podcast, your book, your video series, or whatever your project may be. Add the internal mental encouragement you'll get that comes from having an approach so targeted that you're only buying the best and most relevant items for your desired results.

The feeling you get from undistracted progress is a buzz that even beats two cups of my "special reserve." Truth be told, even if you have to kill the project at some point because you can't answer the questions the way you want to, you will eventually gain some of that same energy from saving yourself additional time and money.

Because, *yes,* you can actually buy the best stuff and still save money, because now everything is relevant to your goals and makes sense in your plan. You are now empowered to make all the right moves because you know what they are, and you know what you want.

And you are empowered to act on it!

And you can do this regardless of how loudly the world is screaming the wrong song at you. When you know why you're doing what you're doing, and exactly what you need to do it, your project, your journey, and your life all go from confusing to amazing.

When you make these four questions part of your process, you can have it all . . .

Constant hope, real clarity, genuine focus, confident direction, minimal waste, enthusiastic empowerment, preferred results, useful energy, motivated fearlessness, and more.

The recipe is already written. It's in this book. The shopping list tells you exactly what you're looking for. Nothing more and nothing less. No more carts full of crap, and the best damn cup of coffee, period.

The 4 Questions

Question 1: What do you want the project to do?

_____

_____

_____

Question 2: How will you know that the project is doing it?

_____

_____

_____

Question 3: Is the project doing it?

_____

_____

_____

Question 4: How can you do it better?

_____

_____

_____

This book is so much more than just four questions.

Scan the QR Code to get access to BONUS material:

Claim Your
Never Go Shopping When You're Hungry

Power Pack: Video Training, Worksheets, and More!

http://NeverShopWhenHungry.com